1

The Wizard of Oz is truly about the path of enlightenment. Advertently or inadvertently, the author uses symbols, allegories and motifs related to ancient sciences. He also uses parody to illustrate, that we are moving into The Age of Aquarius. This is done by making fun of religion. As you may guess, Aquarius is a feminine constellation or zodiac. Thus, the symbols are all feminine to illustrate the goddess concept. Ancient Tarot themes run rampant, to show that The Wizard of Oz is about the journey to enlightenment.   The journey of the Simpleton in the Tarot runs well with this theme, as the female protagonist confronts herself in the person's of the Lion the Tin-man and Scarecrow. Each friend that accompanies Dorothy through her journey represents one of the chakras that the she needs to work on. Notice also that the hero is a female. This is a big move away from the traditional male hero. And finally, the author uses parody to demonstrate the degree of hollow thinking of the Age being replaced. Robotic obedience, hollow body and mind versus independence and self reliance are contrasting themes that pigeonhole the transformation from Pisces to Aquarius.

A lot of people are not aware that the different Ages move in a circular shape, like a spiral. These Ages are characterized by certain energies which affect the public. The energies can only be portrayed as animals because the way animals behave is reminiscent of humans. There is more that can be said about the animalistic nature of the zodiac. But for the sake of brevity, the designer of the zodiac probably had in mind the concept of the role of animals as viewed by indigenous people. In ancient times animals and humans interacted a lot more than now. People who have pets can probable relate to how animals communicate with humans.

So each Age is depicted by a certain totem or animal. In the Age of Leo, a fiery energy is felt. It is documented that a Flood occurred at this time as the ice caps of glaciers melted. We believe this could be the time of "The Lost Continents." The Age of Cancer was matrilineal and people were very spiritual. But many continents sank during there fire and water signs. The Age of Gemini was characterized by communication. Sumeria is chosen as the city that best describe this epoch with all its clay tablets. Egypt with all its beauty would be none other than the Age of Taurus in which bulls and cows were very significant to the people. Moses in the towns of the Israelites destroyed the image of the cow and signified the ram. The story of the ram being caught up in a bush is alluding to the Age of Aries. This epoch was the birth of the Patrilineal system. The One God was observed and thus began monotheism. Akhenaten of Egypt is the original Moses. His real name has Moses in it before he changed it to Akhenaten. Considering how long the Hebrews dwelled in Egypt, it is easy to see where they got their concepts of monotheism from. For some reason, as the Hebrews moved out of Khem or Egypt, the woman was no longer important. Gone were the queens ruling next to their kings. Later as "Christ" or Yashua emerges, we note the fish theme as he beckons fishermen to become fishers of men. This is clear Piscean influence as fish become the order of the day. The ascended Master even turns loaves of bread into fish. To this day we still see symbols of fish on people's cars to denote "Christ." And we even eat fish on Friday to remember Him. Today as we shift to the Age of Aquarius we see more and more Aquarian characteristics. For one, there is the woman's liberation movement that took place. That is not a coincidence. Equality reached, not just the vote arena. After the Civil Rights Movement, the career arena was affected as well. When you think about it, even people's minds are more in tune

2

with the Aquarian personality. The waves you see represent air waves. She pours water from a pitcher. That is one type of wave. But there is also air waves. It is said that Aquarius is an air sign. This brings to mind the air waves of the radio, the wave of the World Wide Web, the microwaves of small ovens and television waves which also involve air. Female energy is characterized by phrases like "let us include everybody," "lets cooperate/form a co-op." We all see the shift, whether slowly or whether it has to be pointed out. Once you see it, you get it. This is very different from the "every man for himself" mentality. Unfortunately, all the baggage from previous Ages has accumulated and we must now heal the planet. War is one such baggage from the age of the Ram, which is ruled by Mars.

A disclaimer must be made at this point. Although the original work uses satire to point out blind faith in a single leader or guru, it in no way demeans people who were born under the sign of Pisces or Aries. The problem being pointed out is that after years of exposure to Mosaic Law and a doctrine that diminishes the power of women, the Piscean Age carries with it baggage. This baggage is not so desirable in the Aquarian Age. So despite Pisceans being super-spiritual or Christ-like, one must wonder the following. Of what avail is spirituality, when part of God is being denied? If everything is everything and if all is in the ALL, then God has both male and female energies. This is true not only historically, but logically and scientifically as well. There is plenty of evidence that women and goddesses have been suppressed. The suppression of women brings back thoughts of witch hunts. The power to see the unseen is indeed feared, even if it manifests as women's intuition.

Frank Baum depicts the concept of the suppression of the female principle in the following manner. He does this by portraying Dorothy as not being heard by Aunt Em or Uncle Henry. This also includes the farm hands. Being that they comprise her world, it seemed to Dorothy that no one was listening. Her every sentence was interrupted and she was being made to feel useless. "Make yourself useful," said Aunt Em. The witch, I mean , Mrs. Gulch is out to get her dog. She has no real job except to get in people's way. This suppressed goddess does not even know who she is. She has no idea she is royalty, but is later treated as such. Meanwhile her instincts tell her to escape, prompted by Aunt Em's instruction to find "a place where there is no trouble." This is where Dorothy begins to dream of heaven or paradise. But is paradise a dream, or did she live that reality in a previous life?

In her dream world Dorothy escapes to a land that is the opposite of her dull Kansas. We are left wondering if this dream was real or imaginary. But as in real life, women go within to find answers. So, there you have it. The protagonist is female in order to bring attention to the fact that we are indeed moving into a Zodiac sign that is female. One truly watches prophecy being fulfilled in real life regarding the 1960's movement and even before that, when women gained voting rights. It makes you wonder if Baum was either a seer or just very knowledgeable about hidden history and science. These suppressed sciences manifest themselves as Dorothy approaches a guru. The Professor Marvel incident also display the idea that going outside of oneself was the modis operandi of the Age of Pisces. The Goddess shows up to make us aware of the transition that is taking place in the heavens. And thus, the comment, as

3

above so below is uttered by Professor Marvel as he quotes Thoth, The Egyptian God that came from Atlantis or Lemuria. Now, this guy had many incarnations. Even Christ incarnated and reincarnated. Being that he said "ye are gods" that means that you can too. But you don't see that. Sad how preachers have lied to us; making us believe the answer is without when it is within. We will find later on that Dorothy is the reincarnation of a very ancient goddess. She also travelled the ethereal plane in her "ship" or merkaba. Mary's Ka and Ba. Ka and Ba are soul and spirit. So, I am describing the Mother Soul and Spirit which some have come to call Mary. But that is another lesson; Ma's Ray of healing comes from the heart. The heart Chakra, that is. Amazing that the heart Chakra is green and healing is green as seen in nature. When animals get sick they eat green. It gets deeper. Some short scenes may illustrate the point. For example, when Dorothy wanted to heal, she searched in nature. Notice the nature themes in the land she woke up in. Flowers, talking trees and butterflies are more than just beautiful. The point is being made that all things turn to nature when they want to heal. In Khem, the ancient name for Egypt, Mother Nature is Neter/Netcher. Actually it's just the other way around. The word for god in Khem is Neter, from which others get the word Nature as in Mother Nature. Aside from the Munchkinland nature scene, we also experience what life is like in the ancient forest full of lions and tigers and bears, not just talking trees.

But short scenes are not the only thing that Frank Baum uses to illustrate his points. The story itself is full of imagery and symbols. The first thing that comes to mind in terms of symbols in the Wizard of Oz is the tornado. Later on we see, the rainbow, the ball of light Spheres, a falling house, talking trees and many others such as the famous yellow brick road. But what do they all mean? And how is this tied to the chakras? To start, the tornado is symbolical of the crisis that occurs to Dorothy when she is not heard. Dorothy tries to tell her family and farm hands about a very important predicament she is in. The only entity that she can relate to, Toto is about to be taken away from her. The fact that no one listens is a demarcation of how women traditionally have been voiceless in times past. To start, the tornado is a female symbol. Anything dealing with water is usually a female symbol. Women have been described as stormy and being overly emotional. The cyclone is a powerful force characteristic of Mother Nature at her most destructive level. This ties into the concept of the dissolution of forms, to emphasize that the old thought patterns of the previous Ages are coming to an end. The message that we must move forward into the Aquarian Age as a force to be reckoned with is clear.

Emotionally speaking, tornados can send you into a whirl, difficult to escape from. And that is exactly what happened to Dorothy when no one paid attention to what she was trying to say. Thus, emotionally, Dorothy was out of alignment as a result of not being heard. The metaphor here is that women's voices have been silenced. It seems the thought pattern started with religion. At some point after goddess worship, women were to be seen and not heard. Dogma taught that women were to obey husbands and never preach. But Dorothy is different. Dorothy is outspoken when the time calls for it. The author seems to be making fun at faith based religious obedience. He takes a stab at authorities that are not questioned and how power corrupts. We are forced to ask ourselves just who put these people in charge. Self appointed gurus and religious authority quickly fall to the wayside once

4

one discovers that one has the answers within ourselves. Our DNA is wired like gods. It is just a matter of introspection.

It seems that Frank Baum is well aware of what the role of women was in ancient times, and how suppressing their natural instinct has led to a meltdown in women. The treatment of women as incapable of intelligence results in lack of self esteem in women. This is exactly what happened to

Dorothy in The Wizard of Oz story.   Dorothy takes on a defeatist attitude. We witness her spirit going from peppy to almost fatalistic. She seems to give up trying to convince people who are not listening. It is this defeatist attitude that sends her in turmoil; a total characteristic of a person who lacks self esteem. Amongst healers, it is well known that the suppression of expression affect the functionality of the chakras.

Dorothy may not realize what was happening to her on the inside as far as her lights becoming dimmer. All she knows is at this point that she wants to escape. There goes that low Chakra defense mechanism of flee or fight. In terms of symbolic language in the movie the first symbol of escape is The Rainbow. Interesting is the fact that the rainbow colors coincide with the colors of the Chakras in the exact order, except it looks like an inverted Chakra. Attention is being brought to the fact that rainbows can be used as a bridge between worlds; the material and the ethereal. It is even shaped like a bridge. The world of what is real or tangible confronts the fantasy or dream world. It also references this Earth and another galaxy or universe or another star system.   With all the reference to the Egyptian or Kemetic sciences, it should not be surprising that Orion is being referenced. The Egyptians have claimed Orion as their original planet. They have even gone as far as aligning their monuments to Orion. The three Pyramids align with Orion's Belt. Two pyramids form a straight line while one is out of line, just like the star system in Orion. The Amazing part is the distance between each and the total correspondence down to the last mathematical equation.

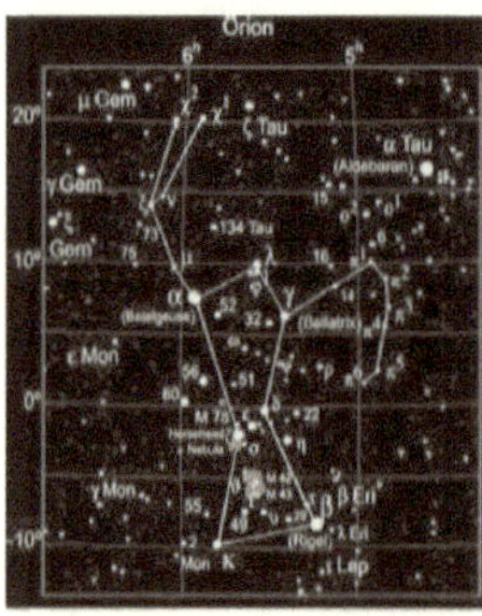

If Dorothy is depicting ancient goddesses, then she must be depicting Innana, who is the most ancient of all goddesses. So ancient is she that she came here as an astronaut from another star system. That star system is Orion. The galaxy or star system is depicted as the Yellow Brick Road which is shaped like spiral or golden mean. This explains why she kept telling everyone that she wanted to go home. Many people cannot comprehend why Dorothy would prefer dull Kansas to colorful Munchkin-Land. The explanation becomes simple once we think of it in terms of being an alien in a planet that is not your own. Possibly Dorothy reached Orion because this has been known as being the home of the gods.

In the true story of Innana, the goddess is stripped off of her jewels. But in the story of Frank Baum Dorothy is stripped of her humanity, which is the same story line. She is not allowed to express herself. In both cases they lose a part of themselves, something precious. The story of Innana sounds quite like the Dorothy character. Here is a helpful quote, "With her right foot Inanna-Ishtar steps on her mascot, a roaring lion, while holding him back on his leash. Between them is Ianna-Ishtar's symbol, the seven-pointed star of the planet Venus. But this is her warrior, not her love goddess aspect. Behind her outspread wings are six bronze weapons or maces, and in her right hand is either a scimitar or a seventh mace. Combined, they may represent the seven "me's" or "laws" that give her power over the Upper World. The printout is over-rolled to produce a symmetrical image around the goddess in the center." Notice that the protagonist holds back the lion, meaning she put her lower desires in check. We see in the movie Dorothy hitting, which equates to putting the lion in check as he tries to bite her dog.

In the ancient story Innana loses her home. In the African reality, Black women lose their humanity by being stripped naked, stripped of their divinity before lustful eyes of mundane men. Many African queens went through this ordeal, though they were of royal lineage. All captured African Queens and those who were already on the continent have in essence, lost their home. Archeology teaches that the most ancient people, including those who landed from outer space, had African features. So was it a dream, a vision, or an altered state of consciousness? Did Dorothy reach Orion?

    If Dorothy is indeed representing Female divinity, this could very well be true. To start, the rainbow is the bridge that bridges two worlds and is seen near the beginning of the story. In the very beginning there is a conflict followed by a storm. Earlier the author mentioned that the time cycles move in circular motions, forming spirals. The cyclone forms this very shape. Escaping conflict is next on the agenda. Consequently, we see Dorothy next crossing a bridge as she decides to run away. The bridge is brilliantly selected shortly after she sings Over the Rainbow. Again running away is an escape mechanism. So it is clear that the author is using the rainbow-bridge analogy to show that realms are crossing.

    But there is more to a rainbow than just symbolizing a bridge between two worlds. Rainbows are a form of light. Each color coincides with the color of the chakras in opposite order. So that red is atop the rainbow, whereas red is at the bottom of the Chakra system. The bottom means foundation. Houses are used to depict foundation. In this case, a foundation has been interrupted by a tornado. Simply put, the tornado is allegory for crisis. Dorothy's foundation has been shook.

    Each ray of the rainbow means something. The red color of the rainbow coincide with root Chakra, orange with the sacrum, yellow with the solar plexus, green with heart Chakra. The heart chakra is green because green is the color of healing. It is the color of nature, and it is what animals eat when they are sick. The most famous healer, Imhotep is called, The Green One. The blue part of the rainbow coincide with the throat Chakra. In The Age of Taurus blue was all the rage. Royal blue or turquoise was used a lot. This is the home of the Diva with the great voice. Venus rules Taurus, so no surprise that there was a lot of emphasis on beauty. Egypt had a lot of information to share with the world. Their throat chakra as a nation was well developed and thus Professor Marvel marvels at their knowledge of sciences, the use of crystal balls and so on. The Eye chakra is colored violet and represents the third eye. The crown chakra is white when not being blocked. "The Crown Heads of Europe" is making reference to the African kings who colonized Europe, namely the Moors. Each European nation has a black face icon wearing a crown as their coat of arms. The Khemites or Blacks in times past were

7

admired for their scientific knowledge. And it is well known that they gave birth to the Renaissance. White light is the light of purity of mind. But the colors of the Chakra are opposite in order to the rainbow. In the rainbow the white light is at the bottom, so you cannot see it with physical eyes unless you are in tune with the cosmos. But that which cannot be seen does not mean it doesn't exist. Comparing the corresponding lights of the bodily Chakras and the rainbow is reminiscent of how the camera inverts light. The human eye itself also acts like a camera, recording every event seen into its own Akashic record. People are born with the records of everything that has happened. They just haven't tapped into it.

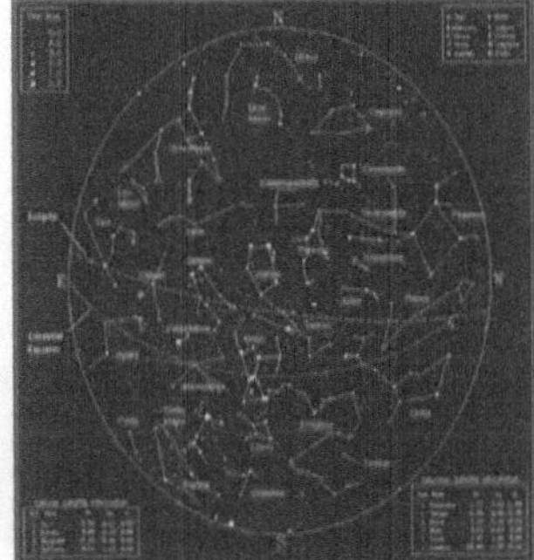

Rainbow signifies how Dorothy travelled from one world to the next, from Earth to Orion, from the world of reality to the world of dreams, from the world of logic to the world of fantasy. In essence, Dorothy astral travelled and here is where the silver slippers come in. The chord that ties one to the astral plane is colored silver, the original color of the ruby slippers. As we dream, we dream in lucid color when we are having a supernatural experience. This means Dorothy's kundalini was activated following a crisis. She went within to find the answers, considering no one else was supplying any answers.

Another way a rainbow is used in ancient times is as a sign that the world will never again be destroyed by water. How does this tie into the Chakra System? We are speaking here of the vibration of color. You must become fluent in the vibration of colors because they correspond to your vehicle. Don't be a machine, be a vehicle. The machine is Tin-man without a heart; whereas a vehicle is a merkaba as one who has ability to fly or astral-travel. We must clear the gateways in order to ascend. One thing that must be left behind is the narrow thinking of those who cut down trees like the unemotional Tin-Man. He represents The Industrial Age. It was at this time that Earth was deforested and de-flowered.

8

The Chakra system is like a machine in that it has wheels. Each chakra frequency correspond to the rainbow, color by color. If used wisely our vehicle could return us home. The 7th Day of Creation correspond with the 7 colors of the rainbow and the 7 chakras. For example, the root chakra corresponds to the root race, whereas the crown chakra is for the race to come in the 7th Day of Creation. Since Dorothy belongs in the 7th Day of creation, she must clean or align each chakra by facing her problems and fears head on. This includes facing lions, tigers and bears. Dorothy gains her voice back in the end when she tells the Wizard of Oz exactly what is on her mind.

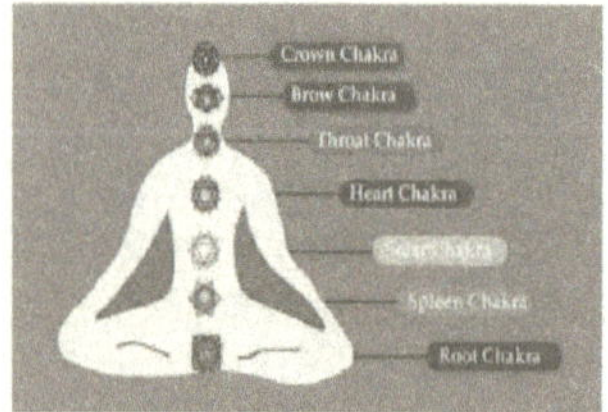

Light spheres are seen as she enters Munchkinland. These spheres seen near Dorothy and near Glinda represent being enlightened. As Dorothy makes peace with herself and aligns her chakra she sees the light figuratively speaking. Yet literally when you bring up your kundlini aka your tornado, you pass through gates and light up your crown using your third eye. The gates in the movie are shown at key points in Dorothy's development. The house has a picket fence or gate, then there's the gatekeeper and so on. Here is a helpful quote about Innana aka Ishtar and the significance of gates, " When Inanna arrives at the first of the seven gates of Kur (the Sumerian Hell), she is challenged by the gate keeper, Neti, to prove her ID and her purpose. But her answer makes no sense to him." Doesn't this sound eerily like the Wizard of Oz story when the male Gatekeeper asks for Dorothy's identification? African-Americans in a like manner have lost their identity and cannot answer the simple question that anyone of other ethnicities can answer, "WHO ARE YOU?" Not by a coincidence, the Wizard asks the same question to Dorothy and her friends. Gatekeepers are the people that keep you from developing spiritually, by denying you access to the mysteries. These people exist in real life. They are called Secret Societies or hoarders. Then there are the Fence Straddlers, who cannot make up their minds like the scarecrow. They won't go in yet keep you from going in when it comes to new knowledge.

Whether you are a Fence Straddler, an illuminati wanna- be, or have reached balance; here is one truth. Each person has a different aura color depending on their level of growth. You will notice that the witch was surrounded by a light. But its color was red like the low level root chakra that she represents. If you are not grounded as a house, you may not ascend. On the other hand if your aura is violet, you are considered well developed. If it is yellow, you are a teacher or wise.

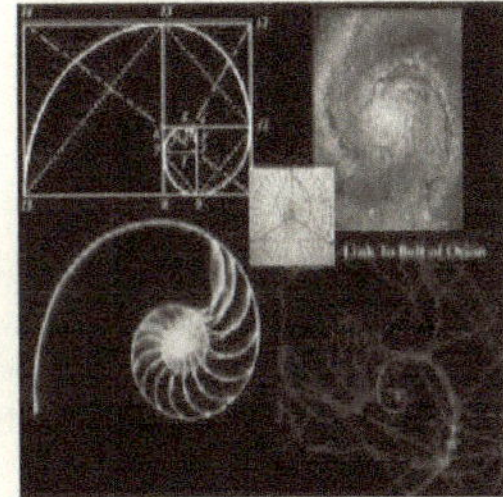

Therefore, it is not a coincidence that the road that leads to wisdom, the Wiz, is yellow. Yellow also represents the sun, a sunny disposition is happy, the opposite of depressed as Dorothy was. Her friend the Scarecrow was always happy and this is what she is aligning herself with. The Golden mean is yellow. Thus you can see the comparisons being made here. The Golden Mean is the ultimate symbol of wisdom. It is also tied to beauty. This is why

Leonardo Da Vinci and others used the Golden Mean to draw their art. Perfection is beauty. And if you measure a human being, the results are the Golden Mean.

Venus is tied to the Golden Mean, another symbol of Beauty or goddess figure. The path of Venus forms a 5 pointed star. S does the Vitruvian Man. These are some of the facts that tie Dorothy to the Golden Mean. Quickly, we see the connection between Dorothy and the Goddess Venus. Dorothy starts her journey at the beginning. And what begins a universe is the Golden Mean. This is even more evidence that a goddess principle is being depicted here.

Another goddess symbol we see is the hourglass. Women are shaped like hourglass. Dorothy looks at the hourglass after the witch tells her she is running out of time. Indeed we are at a time when little time is left for ascension. We are reaching 2012 which is zero point. So the hourglass is depicting the waist or midpoint in the great Cycle of the 12 Ages. Each Zodiac rules every 2,160 years. A zodiac year =25,920. So we at Aquarius are at midpoint, a time of spiritual ascension. That is why Dorothy says the hourglass is almost empty. We are at the 7th level of evolutionary development. And 7 is the midpoint

when you consider there are really 13 signs of the Zodiac. Recent observation shows that Ophiucus was the 13th Sign. This serpent holder was none other than Imhotep the medicine man.

It appears that we are approaching the 7th Day of Creation. A thousand days to the Lord is the equivalent to a man's day a (mere 24 hours). The hours are divided into 24 and Imhotep could be the 24th Elder. So the Lord's Day, the Sabbath makes reference to a Great Year in thousands. Aquarius is that 7th level if you look at the totality of the Zodiac in terms of Great Ages. When the sun was in Leo during the Leo Great Age, the sun's hot rays melted the ice on the glaciers which lead to the Flood in Atlantis during The Golden Age. Naturally the color of Leo being the sun sign would be yellow thus age called golden. The Age of Cancer was a time of a Matriarchal society. Not sure if this was a Lemurian Age but it was female. Cancer is a water sign. Age of Gemini Sumer, communication was its mark. Geminis are great communicators. Writing reached its peak in this Age. The Age of Taurus was the Age of Great Beauty as Venus rules Taurus. The Pyramids, and Temples of Abu Symbal, Luxor, Columns were wrought with beauty. The limestone casings where amazing when the sun shone on it. Science and math were indeed developed but that came from the Age of Leo as everyone knows Atlantis was the ultimate depiction of Wisdom (yellow) and Egypt is a place where Atlantians settled. It has been suggested that Atlantians are other- wordly. Egyptians claim Orion as their homeland. The Dogon also claim Orion and The Dog Star , which is Toto aka Anubis guiding through the underworld. That being said , it is possible that Dorothy travelled to Orion as she astral travelled. In that sense, she did go HOME, or at least, a place like it. Once she got there she saw a lot of strange stuff along with a lot of beauty. Most people want to know why did Dorothy chose Kansas over beautiful Munchkinland or Emerald city for that matter. After all, both places were wrought with abundance. Abundance by the way is another characteristic of The Great Mother.

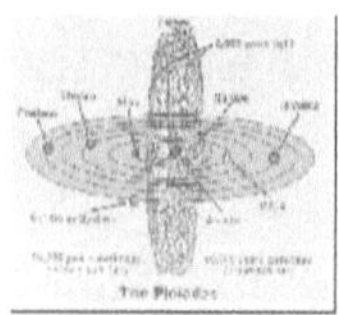

The truth is Kansas is Kansas + Oz. Put them together and you have KansOz or conscious. When Dorothy returns to Kansas she returns to consciousness. And who amongst us wants to be stuck in a dream or another dimension. It is natural to want to get back into your body after astral travel.   This is why she was being told to tap her shoes to get back home. In other words you must tap into your subconscious in order to align the Chakra System. We must then tap into our subconscious dreams to find answers. We must rely on ourselves when we do this. This is why the emphasis on self reliance.

Trees, flowers, butterflies, streams in Munchkinland are all symbols of the Divine Feminine as well as Mother Nature. Thus we see literally with our own eyes, the theme of female divinity. The protagonist in this story is female. This is a hint that we are dealing with the return of the Divine Feminine. We see talking trees to emphasis a communion with Mother Nature. Females seem to be more in tune with Mother Nature. Dorothy even talks to dogs. All cultures emphasize goddesses affiliation with nature. We see it in Demeter, Persephone, Minerva, and all ancient goddesses. Mother as having a womb is depicted as a circle, the opposite of a square. The cellar is a hole to depict going into the womb during time of turmoil or cyclone. The fire aura is circular. Glinda's light is circular. The Yellow Brick Road starts out as circular. All beginnings are circular. An embroyo is circular at birth. Eggs are circular. No surprise that chicks are in the movie during a talk of fertility and lack thereof. There is a fertility problem at the end just as predicted in the Bible, women will stop having babies or have problems with fertility. This is true in today's society of fertility clinics. Whether it is due to abortions or chemicals the problem is there. Test tube babies have become a reality. Removal of uterus is emphasized nowadays for any cysts.   Instead of removing the problem they remove the uterus. Why not just chew lemons? The removal of the uterus is reminiscent of removal of the circle on an ankh which is the womb itself. This predicament resulted in the cross, which is an ankh without its head, the mother. Dorothy is seen at the

12

crossroads. She seemed to be asking, "Which way do you go?" There is confusion at the end because the female head , which is the Matriarch or goddess has been removed or forgotten. It is this mentality that a parody is made of, not so much a Piscean mentality. Pisceans are very spiritual. That age did give birth to Christ or Buddha or The Light of the World. But each Age carries baggage from a previous Age. So there was a lot of father god figure mentality that carried on to Piscean Age. This is why Christ's disciples did not understand why he was surrounded by women or why Mary Magdalene was told secrets that the others did not receive. The Christed alluded to the Aquarian Age to follow by saying "follow the man with the pitcher (of water). Scarecrow seems to be crucified at the crossroads. If he is another Christ symbol, then he must be depicting Black man who has been crucified by the literal definition of the word, which is to castrate. Scarecrow represents the Ayn or Eye, the Eye of God, the Third Eye. The all-seeing Eye that solves all the problems. He seems to have the answer to everything. His self esteem issue is no different than any oppressed person. The Lion, too seem to have these issues. And let us not forget Tin-Man who has become as cold as the Age of Industry he represents. The Age of Industry is more like the Age of the Slave. Thus we see slave themes throughout this movie.

Allusions to ancient sciences run rampant to emphasize a return to the ancient ways. At some point we started going to gurus, then preachers and now we need to return to ourselves. "To be or not to be" so dependent is the real question. Outside forces cannot solve our problems as we saw with Katrina. This is part of the Aquarian Age thinking. It is an Age of Freedom. Professor Marvel speaks of the Crown Heads of Europe. These are the people who had developed their Crown Chakra, which is the ultimate goal. Professor Marvel uses a crystal ball. Our skulls have crystals and pyramids in them. That is what the crystal ball symbolizes. And this is where the crystal skull divinatory system comes from. Earth Crystals also help align the Chakra System. And you can communicate with them. Ancient knowledge has been stored in them.

13

Eventually evil entered the world and this caused the closing of the Third Eye. Only certain people were able to access the world of nature using certain plants. This gave birth to shamans as intermediaries between Nature and humanity. Same happened with preachers or religious figures as intermediaries. But now that thinking is over. There are no more middle men; only the ones you allow to fool you. The Age of Aquarius is here to say that we need to get back into depending on self. Today you hear the echo of that philosophy in songs such as The Greatest Love, and Aquarius Let The Sunshine In. "the greatest love of all is inside of me…I decided long ago never to walk in anyone's shadow if I fail if I succeed at least" then at least you can't blame anyone else. "Harmony and understanding, sympathy and trust abounding, no more choices that cause derision (no one can make fun of us anymore) golden living dreams of visions (golden as the yellow brick road, the Golden Mean) mystic crystal revelation (crystal skulls)." The song by The 5th Dimension makes reference to the crystal city being inside you. The Emerald City is inside you. We have crystal inside our head. Computers mimic these crystals and are able to get information on the spot. The computer is a technology straight from The Age of Aquarius. It is all inclusive. Everyone can benefit, not just the few such as the elite or chosen few. It includes the whole. "And the minds true liberation –Aquarius." It seems like they chose the right title for their group and song as well. Aquarius: Let The Sunshine in. The sun shining in is making reference to you becoming enlightened.

Aquarius is the mind's true liberation because prior to that Age, we were under the impression that answers were outside of us. We would go to gurus (the professor marvels), shamans, religious figures wizards, Moses, god's representative, preachers, pastors, Yoruba priests and the like. Dorothy as Return of Divine Feminine kills the witch with water. Right there she is showing that she is The Water Bearer. The Angel that is androgynous is neither male nor female. It represents the alchemy, the marriage of merging male and female energies. Lord knows Dorothy had both. She was courageous from the start and aggressive by standing up to Mrs. Gulch when her surrogate parents were too afraid to. The water Bearer is the symbol of Aquarius. This has various meanings. Water dissolves. It represents the dissolution of forms. The forms are antiquated belief systems where the male had to exercise control and literally dominated by control and manipulation. This wizard or illusionist was able to control only because he was a clever enough wizard to get us into thinking that the ultimate god is male and that there is no female divinity. We believe this mentality came about due to fear of the unknown. This is speaking about the fear of the unknown powers of the female. Men wonder how can women know? How does she reach the Akashic records? Dorothy reached the Akashic records; opposite of Kansas. Kansas represents the conscious mind. She did this by tapping into the unconscious mind. Thus was able to solve all her problems. She connected to the lion's paw. The Giza Pyramid holds the Akhashic record. The Lion's golden color makes allusion to Golden Age when Leo reigned as well as the Golden Mean I might add. So, this is not to say women are superior. It is saying that both male and female are equally potent, equally smart, and can be equally courageous. And of course, they both have a heart. They each just need to learn how to use these powers. Courage is masculine. Women need to use their male energies wisely and not give in feebly or give up. Males need to develop a heart so that they can be balanced and stop all the wars. Testosterones are just as out of balance as a hysterical female on her

14

period...so which is worst? None is better. They all are energies operating at the lowest levels. If we each work on our virtue, then we would reach wisdom. That is the message of the Sphinx. The Sphinx is a composite of animals. The protagonists of the Zodiac are the fixed constellations, starting with the lion, who was here from the beginning. Had he not abused his power, he still would be king. Then there is the stubborn bull, who sees with the Eye of God. It is now shifting Gemini though as we experience The Shift. And that's why so much emphasis on the twins (Twin Towers, Twin Pillars, original Twins Adam and Eve and so forth). Next is Scorpio who has dealings with an eagle represented by the wings of the Sphinx, which was taken down to symbolize the loss of spirituality or the loss of spirit or the loss of flight. And finally there is the human. This is The Water Bearer, Aquarius. And yes there was an ancient female Sphinx, Innana. But we must understand that female principles and male principles are not gender specific. That's why angels are depicted as androgynous. They are balanced meaning, they don't go to the polar extreme. Go to any extreme and you find it is one and the same; just opposite of same coin.

It is clear that The Wizard of Oz is speaking to the hearts of those who can relate to the Innana story. For example, Innana is asked the following by the gatekeeper, ""If you are truly Inanna, Queen of Heaven, On your way to the East, Why has your heart led you on the road From which no traveler returns?" In the Wizard of Oz, Dorothy is travelling east considering she has killed The Wicked Witch of the West. Both are on a journey to the East. The East is known as being more spiritual than The West. They are both trying to get back to their higher selves. Dorothy is seeking wisdom but she has to pay a heavy price for it. She must get the Broom of the Witch of the East. In The Innana story, Innana holds the 7 MEs. This to me is just another way of saying, she has conquered her lower self as she demonstrates by taming the lion and the 7 MEs are her 7 chakras. Each Chakra represents a gland. So, the body is divided into 7 parts. Each person has a twin soul, so together there are 14 divided parts that we must come to terms with. It is easier to ascend with your other half. Sound familiar? Does it begin to sound like the Isis/Auset story?

Speaking of ascension the following needs to be read carefully because here we see allusions to The Emerald City;

"My Queen, a maid
As tall as heaven,
As wide as the earth,
As strong as the foundations of the city wall,
Waits outside the palace gates.
She has gathered together the seven me.
She has taken them in her hands.
With the me in her possession, she has prepared herself:
On her head she wears the shurgarra, the crown of the steppe.
Across her forehead her dark locks of hair are carefully arranged.
Around her neck she wears the small lapis beads.

At her breast she wears the double strand of beads.
Her body is wrapped in the royal robe.
Her eyes are daubed with the ointment "let him come, let him come."
Around her chest she wears the breast plate called "come, man, come!"
On her wrist she wears the gold ring.

The city wall brings our eyes to the first view of The Emerald City. It mentions her having to wait outside the gate. Here she is, royalty, and is made to wait. The last shall be first. Dark locks refer to her being African in ethnicity, the very people who started the locking their hair in ancient times. She wears the crown on her head just as the fairy godmother did. In other words, she has arrived in more ways than one. She has come into her own in this Aquarian Age of the Divine female energy. Not surprisingly, she is made up with make up around eyes just as in The Wizard of Oz Dorothy is made up. The Egyptians wore kohl around their eyes to symbolize being awoke or waking to the Eye of Re. The Reyes or Rays of the Dark Black Sun. That is just too many coincidences for it to be accidental. Why do they dress Dorothy all up and give her the royal treatment? Because once she is ID'd at the gate, she is identified (EYE-DENTified) and they find that she is royal indeed. She is The Queen of Heaven! She is Innana. The story of Cinderella all dolled up at the gate has been the story of the African American female. In fact, German soldiers and other European soldiers heard the story in its origin. And that is why Cinderella is sooted with Black chimney dust – to portray her Blackness. But they had to speak in codes because of the persecution. The persecution involved, the Inquisition, Jim Crow and before that, The Crusades, including he so-called Crucifixion. The crucifixion is none other than the Tarot Card of The hanged Man. He is the one who got lynched and all his riches were stolen, represented by the coins coming out his pocket. His world literally turned upside-down once his queen was taken from him. One can only think of the glory of the Moors and their effect as initiators of European Rennaissance. We all know that when the "Jews/Yahudas and Moors and Muslims were expelled from Spain, their gold and resources were taken from them. That is what the Tarot - Open Book of the Bible was trying to tell you. The Bible is the Coming Forth By Day, basically, The Book of The Dead. Bab- El, Gateway to Heaven, Door of The Gods. These were just some of the gems taken from the Moors. Moors are depicted blindfolded with heads cut off to show they lost their third eye. The crucifixion shows up again as the lynching as they hang from trees. It has been said that one who hangs on a tree is cursed and this is why they did it. This is part of the magic used against them. Magic was used against the female, too. The following is true.

"This is not a picture of a pretty younger sister all dolled up and decked out in her finest finery. This isn't Cinderella at the palace gates, ready for the ball. This is the Queen of Heaven. And she is as tall as Heaven. And strong as a wall. And (three times the gate-keeper repeats for emphasis) she is armed with the seven me, the powers of her rule over the upper world. She is, quite literally, dressed to kill. She wears a stunning hair-do, gleaming eye paste, and a dazzling display of jewelry, Not mere baubles, but man-killing allure, and the gate-keeper feels their power. And, finally, this: "

Now read it again and picture Dorothy at the Gate, being prepared/made up with eye paste as well. And the hair was done too. Reference to the wall bring to mind the Tower, which

16

represents strength. She is Mary Magdalene in a sense as Christ's Bride in the sense that she is the partner of the crucified mate and this time her amygdale has been sparked or initiated.

See the picture below and does it not remind you of a Sphinx? It is well known that Dorothy and her friends represent just that. The four fixed signs and their power at the end.

So as you can see from the old paint her wings were black like the ravens in the story of Dorothy and the Scarecrow scene. Innana's lion also had a black haired mane. This is finally the black haired lion that is so elusive. And this confirms the truth that when these royal travelers brought the lion, the original mane was black! Now Blacks in Africa paint their bodies red all the time with clay. The Blacks in the West did the same thing. There were no red people, just Blacks covered in red paint. They call her Lillith in contempt, but we know who she is.

20 centuries before Christ, Mesopotamians carved this clay plaque of the goddess Lilith. Paint traces show her body was red and her wings black, the colors of blood and death. The owls' feathers alternated red and black, and the lions' manes were black.

To me she may have been the true original Sphinx. Notice the flying creature apparatus or outfit. The ancient writings continue to mention the lapis lazuli around her neck and hands. Dorothy wears a lapis lazuli colored outfit. This is the regalia of ancient royal lineage. The ruby slippers are the clawed feet regalia that have power over life and death. Scorpio is the agent associated with eagle and read about it's relationship to death. The witch could not take off Dorothy's shoes/slippers. As she said, "these things have to be done delicately." Then she adds, "or it might hurt the spell," proving that a spell was cast over African Americans and all melanated peoples. Too much information revealed might cause them to wake up. That is why The Templars / gatekeepers wrote things in codes. As Margaret Starbird said, the left hand was used to indicate the female. But she never came out and said the royal lineage is speaking of Black people. But I read between the lines whether she meant it advertently or not. Whether Margaret Starbird was aware that every great person is tied to Blacks I do not know. But those with eyes to see and ear to hear can simply pick up the clues and put the pieces of the puzzle together.

Here is another interesting quote to remind us of the witch who betrayed Dorothy.

When Ereshkigal heard this,
She slapped her thigh and bit her lip.
She took the matter into her heart and dwelt on it.
Then she spoke:
'Come, Neti, my chief gatekeeper of the kur,
Heed my words:
Bolt the seven gates of the underworld.
Then, one by one, open each gate a crack.
Let Inanna enter.
As she enters, remove her royal garments.
Let the holy priestess of heaven enter bowed low.'
The 7 gates here refers to those lower drives below the high virtuous, 7 in

all. The 7 virtues include charity love etc. This is what you strive for to become a whole person. However, when Eve got seduced by the serpent, she turned those energies into the 7 deadly sins which include, hate, envy lust, fear laziness and so on. The scarecrow was too lazy to use brain. There is no virtue in that. The lion was too cowardly to come unto his own, confusing intelligence with fear when outnumbered. In other words, they lived in fear of The Man, who turned out in the end to be a sham....a user of stolen ancient wisdom. Everyone bows to The Man, but all people have to do is pull the curtain to see that he is. The man behind the curtain is bogus and has no power over you. The only true power is your power and no one can take that away.

Notice in the above quote that Innana is stripped off of her jewels "one by one." One Chakra after another, one power center after another until she becomes like the beast man or beast of the field,

18

blind to her divinity and naked. "And remove her royal garments..." This occurred when Africans were stripped naked off their royal regalia...the headdresses, the crown of Lower Egypt, The Crown of Upper Egypt and many other headdresses of Kings of Mali, Queens of Ghana, Somalia, Sudan and many others were taken down. Those of us who study esoteric knowledge know that the crowns of Egypt were crowns that represent the thymus gland and other glands that help you elevate or ascend if you will. It is even shaped like one. So many similar events occurred on many levels because as above so below. In other words, whatever happens on the cosmic level manifest itself on the microcosmic level. What happens to the sun affects us. What happens to the moon affects us. Innana was made to enter "The Underworld," – the world of the lower realms of existence, the material world. The mundane world of materialism was shoved down African Americans throats until they lost sight of their own culture. They were stripped naked for all to see with eyes of lust. It was this lust that drove them to close their third eye. These are the 7 lower MEs spoken of in this passage. And with the passage of time the new rite of passage was being split apart by horses running in opposite direction as one is tied in middle, being tarred and so on. The true rite of passage was lost. Their eyes were closed. The serpent people lied to them. They were told that their eyes would open but they taught just the opposite. Indigenous people do not lust after naked people. This is only seen in European culture. And so Africans learned lust after being exposed to serpent people. This is an aspect of the closing of the third eye. Now these same people are having to learn all over again how to clear the Chakras aka the Kabbalistic Tree or Cabbala.

A servant man is in charge of Innana's being stripped of her clothing. The mere servant is the slave aka the Slavonic people from which derived the word slaves. Gate by gate she goes, being stripped. Each gate represents a Chakra. They literally wanted to turn her into an animal, a cattle. This is the exact term that the Europeans used to describe African Americans "cattle." Oh, and what a coincidence, there are 7 gates in the Innana story. Later we see in the Dorothy story the slave theme.

"In any case, at the first gate Inanna loses her crown; at the second her lapis necklace, at the third and sixth her breast beads; at the fourth her breast plate; at the fifth her wrist ring; at the sixth her measuring rod and line; and at the seventh her royal robe. [In the Akkadian version, the last thing to go is her loincloth]."

As you read the above quote, notice that each item removed correspond to the location of a Chakra. Crown, Brow/third eye, throat, heart solar plexus, sacral and root. Let your imagination run wild, the root and loin cloth go hand in hand. Read on, not surprisingly she was judged by those who stripped her and hung on a hook on the wall. The Dutch hung Africans on hooks. Hmn. This alludes to the lynchings as Africans hung on trees after being stripped of their royalty literally and symbolically. All of this is followed by the usual bragging which persists to this day:

"Here is Ashurnasirpal II, in 877, bragging how he tortured and displayed the corpses of his enemies:

"I built a pillar by the city gate and I flayed all the chiefs who had revolted, and I covered the pillar with their skin. Some I walled up within the pillar, some I impaled upon the pillar on stakes, and others I bound to stakes around about the pillar..."

The bragging continues just as it does today,

'It seems he skinned them alive. Here he brags of other tortures:

"I burned many captives. From some I cut off their noses, their ears and their fingers, of many I put out the eyes. I made one pillar of the living and another of heads, and I bound their heads to tree trunks round about the city. Their young men and maidens I burned in the fire..."
(Quoted by John and Elizabeth Romer, The Seven Wonders of the World, p 121.)'

This is reminiscent of being tarred and applied molten lead to and so on as it happened to African Americans, Blacks in the Caribbean, Moors, Brazilians, Black Jews and dark people period.

In this day and time floods and tsunamis are destroying cities. Fires are destroying the world in the form of gun-powders, bombs, airplanes crashing into buildings. Duality is being killed. Duality thinking from the Age of Pisces where fishes are swimming apart is not helping us evolve anymore. It is time for a change. The change is usually inevitable at the crossroads of a new age. The Galactic Cross is calling us to pay attention to the oneness that Aquarian thinking brings. Aquarius thinks in oneness as in One Nass = One People.

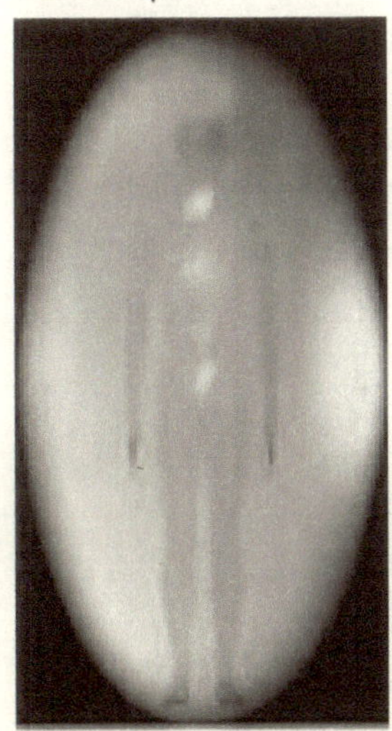

20

The lion in his lower state proves that he represents her lower Chakra, the root Chakra. By biting Toto or trying to and wagging his tail, he is demonstrating primal instincts. The root Vhakra rule primal instincts to include flee or fight. Dorothy says "I will BITE you myself you wicked old witch." Name-calling and biting and aggression are all properties of root chakra when it is imbalanced. The fear that the lion displays, as he repeats, "I do believe in ghosts, I do I do I do I do," is but one example of how fears manifest in your reality. Fear is induced by the magic of the screen TV among many other magic tricks. The witch caught a whiff of his fear because she too has access to the Akasha by the use of magic. It may be cheating, but it is access nevertheless. The same way animals pick up your fears. It is important to keep fear in check because as you can see, it can be used against you. This is an example of the need to align the sacral chakra to its proper state.

Dorothy is just as out of alignment as the lion in his lowly state. Her heart is out of line when she lets her dog attack the cat on a regular basis. Then she has the nerve to say "he doesn't do it every-day, just once or twice a week." It never should be done. That is totally unacceptable. Even though Mrs. Gulch represents the monopolists thinking from ages past such as Aries and Pisces mentality, she had a right to defend her cat. Although I cannot agree that she should take their entire farm. Either way, Dorothy's heart is out of line and thus she needs to align her heart chakra. That is where the Tin-man comes in. Though he claims not to have a heart, he cries all the time, which goes to show he does have a heart. The Tin-man represents to a certain degree that ray of the sun, the green ray which happens to be the ray of the heart. He has the capacity to ove. He just doesn't know it yet.

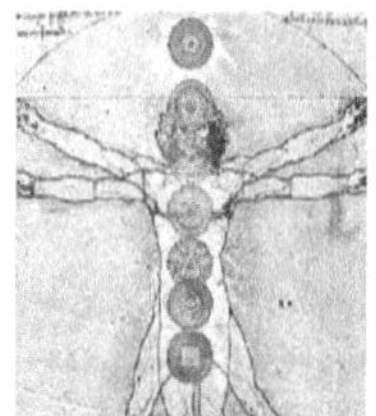

Buy Dorothy continues to make the same mistake over and over, going by Mrs. Gulch's garden (another mother Earth symbol). This shows she is not using her brain and is in need of aligning her wisdom chakra. That's where scarecrow comes in. He represents the eye Chakra. He also represents yellow, the color of wisdom.

We are witnessing a dichotomy: slavery/ dependence versus freedom. This is a result of the shifting of the ages. Best way to combat the downside is to become perfectly aligned and single eyed [John 17:11]. It's what The Master meant when he said, "let thine eye be single." Some people are rebelling against the change because they simply believe in tradition.

21

Only an out of balance mind can deny Mother. A mother brings you into life and to deny her is to demonstrate the thinking of the time. Christ said follow the man with the pitcher. In other words, follow what the Aquarian Age is telling you. The Age of Aquarius brings together the mentality of Christ Consciousness. The Master also said," Ye are gods" [John 10:34]. The master KRST also said, "The Kingdom of God is within." Look within. Be self- reliant like Dorothy. That is what The Age of Aquarius is all about; access the Akasha or God through the unconscious. The Akasha can also be accessed through dream time or astral travel, not just through meditation. People now mimic that process through the internet, an age of waves or the sign of air. That is why He said, "There shall be no sign given to you," because air is nothing – NO- THING. The air sign of Aquarius is manifestation is micro-waves, radio waves, television waves, and world wide web. All these are all air technology. Depicted as water Bearer symbol of connecting the Piscean water sign with air sign of Aquarius air waves and wavy lines are female energy. No sense in denying female energy because when you do, you enslave self and others. The little people become enslave in a monotheistic society.   Women are known as chatterboxes so no surprise about the communication part of it.

There has to be a trinity. People become enslaved in a society of male dominance where dictators reign...the same thing happens in an aristocracy and oligarchy. The few expand and benefit at the hands of a few. The Munchkins are the little people that suffer. The rest of us are the peons or little people, at least in their eyes. But David slew Goliath. And Judy slew the witch. Each used an unassuming instrument. The little people of the forest can also represent the indigenous people who work around nature not against it. The sleepy heads are babies, to represent the childlike quality of those who want to come into Christ consciousness. They cry out, "this is their day of independence," as liberation themes run rampant. Notice how fearful they are at first. Post traumatic syndrome causes this seemingly irrational fear. They want to make sure wickedness is really dead. When Blacks were emancipated, many could not believe it and were still dwelling in the plantation.

Another way that dependency is emphasized as depicting the shift from one age to another is the way the denizens of Emerald city are portrayed. They are portrayed as being overly dependent. "Dorothy! Who is Dorothy? Let's ask the Wizard, he knows." Yea the wizard has the answer to everything and thus they are misled. He is misleading the people by turning himself into a god that he is not. The white pope does this. They call him father and he supposedly blesses people. He turns out to be a sham, a humbug just like the Wizard. The sham is another word for a sun meaning he is wise he is just not a very good wizard. This happens to men in modern day, the preachers, who claim to be a go –between – a mediator between mankind and God. Symbols of the church are readily seen in the arch-way that are prevalent in the Emerald city or the city of the Wizard. Religion has turned out to be a sham because it mixes a lot of truths with lies.

The next symbol is The Field of Poppies. Many people associate poppies with hallucinogens. But there is a double meaning. While it is true that some shamans gain access to the Akasha, field of poppies mean we have fallen asleep. We have fallen asleep to our true nature. We have forgotten who we are and what we are capable of. Our skills lie dormant chiefly due to the way illusionists are

22

misguiding us. It is as though we are ruled by a magic spell from which we can't seem to be able to wake up from. The spell is so bad and deeply rooted with indoctrination of misguidance i.e. patriarch false notion that women should not be heard that it would take divine intervention to get us out of this plight. You can tell a spell exists, by the way some people worship everyone except themselves. It has been said that the small percentage of people that rule the world do so through a magic spell where they have put people to sleep. In true life that seems to be true when you consider the secret societies ruling and their belief in magic. There are also chemicals in the water deliberately put there to dumb people down. Sodium-Fluoride is one such compound. Vaccination with mercury is another method used. The foods are full of chemicals and approved by FDA aka the powers that be.

The only way to wake up from this spell is to stop being so dependent on the system. We must remove ourselves from the false Matrix and embrace The True Matriarch. Dorothy is seeking answers and as she goes within, she accesses The Divine Mother. Some say she made contact with her higher self. Others say God herself came to the rescue of an orphan. There is that Cinderella motif. Mother Earth/Divine Mother gently guides Dorothy with love. She shows up in the form of a fairy godmother, Glinda. Her glow of light shows that she is divine, and associated with royalty, possibly a Mary figure. This Mary figure is associated with The Empress. Her crown has 6 pointed stars just like the Empress. This makes her possibly the woman clothed with the sun spoken of in the Bible. She is no other than the Empress of the Tarot. Either Mary Mother of God herself has come to the rescue, or Dorothy has accessed her higher self. Both statements can be true if we are all one. The royal path is saying accomplish your mission in life by being the best possible person you can be. Get a handle of those lower base desires, those negative attributes that keeps us lazy and keeps us enslaved to a monopolistic elite. Wake up and ascend. Rise above the old mentality and be your own person like Dorothy. The witch's castle is surrounded by negative eyes, red bloodshot eyes in the owl, the Vulcan all goes to show these people have fallen and some of them are working as agents [i.e. agent Smith, the original smiths were blacksmiths]for the matrix such as the flying monkeys. Original black people who were once known for their royalty, are now dependent on a wicked system that exploits them. They have melanin- the ability to fly. You can see it in their pre-Greek hairstyles which is African.

The hairstyle of the flying monkey is telling us, it is speaking of Africans. These are the people who imitate Masa and follow the false master at every whim. These are the agents that work for their adversary's government period. They don't think they have a chance in the world of making it on their own. They work against their own people but only because they are not using their brains to forge creativity. Others simply are not using logic. But once they bring their left brain together with their right brain, they will be able to be single eyed and thus self dependent.

And then there are those who do not necessarily work for the system of agents, but they just haven't found their way yet. They have the brain-power but have not put it to use. You may find them in jails though they are geniuses. Locked in a cell they find themselves, only to find in the end, that the key was

25

in plain sight. They don't see it because of indoctrination and programming. The sad part is, most don't know they have been programmed or how. Perhaps they are looking at the wrong crystal, such as the tell lie vision (television). Television has crystals built into it. But that is just one tool. There are many other tools of those who chain the royal bloods. In the age when the story of Oz was written and even now, many blacks remain "straw-man," suffering from lack of self-esteem. We know slavery did this to them. It is well depicted in the munchkin scenario where fear rules and themes of slavery reign as they shout about captivity and independence. Truthfully, like Judy, they have the answer all along but they just don't know it yet. And you can't tell them that, they have to find it for themselves (like Dorothy). The human looking agents are no different in terms of using the brain. With a dumb sounding tone the witch's agent says, " you killed her!" This reminds me of dumb military and police that enforce a wicked system.

When Dorothy sings, "You could be another Lincoln, if you only had a brain," this seals the message that Blacks who were once royal pharaohs and are now slaves, are being addressed. Lincoln being the so-called emancipator is figuratively speaking of course. For the sake of argument, she is saying, thinking can lead your people to freedom if you use your mind wisely.

The fall came about because the wrong people ate the Tree of Knowledge. The tree of knowledge means they ate up information, ransacked the Library of Alexandria, used technology to kill and dissect. But what profiteth a man to gain the whole world and lose his soul? The tree

with apples in the movie represents the Tree of knowledge. They should
have eaten the Tree of Life. This means they should have embraced
life. Instead, they killed the planet by chopping trees like the heartless Tin-
man. The Tin-man is half robot and half human. How much more
emotionless can you get than a robot? They make Earth sick with their
technology. So now Mother Earth has come herself as a Savioress. She is
the prodigal daughter who returns home. It is a journey to return to your
roots or how things were in the beginning. So is she a good witch or a bad
witch? People are as ugly as they behave. This witch fairy higher self lesson
teaches us that we all have power. Used in the wrong way, it can destroy
and be destroyed, but power used correctly can give life and empower
others.

Smoke around the Wizard shows the pompous ways of the church, just
one big show and no real spirituality. People shout, pretending to feel the
spirit, but it is so phony. One sees and hear preachers shouting, screaming
trying to sound important and the crowd says hallelujah as if he said
something deep, typical mindless indoctrination. Pomp is not the only
problem with religious figures. Another problem is control. Religion is a tool
to control. Dumbed down, the mindless people run around lost and
dependent. Forcing one to follow a mediator is just another form of
control. Religions tell people where to sit, when to enter, when to exit and if
not careful they will tell you when you can be allowed to go to the
bathroom. You must wait for a certain break in the program before you can
go to the bathroom or leave or enter. If you come late you must wait for a
break in the song or sermon before you can enter. This control freak
attitude is a turn off and keeps people from getting to God. The top people
are rich. The members are poor. The poor members seldom get the help
they need, but are asked to give, give and give. Religion is a sham; and it's
easy to see through the pomp just to make

26

preachers rich. Religious people molest people, participate in violence and
dog women. When will people wake up. Now if you speak spirituality that is
different. Spiritual people are ethical. Religious people are con men. This
includes members who are only interested in casting spells on their
enemies, which is everybody. They become happy when bad things happen

to their enemies and call themselves peacemakers and Christians. Right.
They are witches and warlocks. And thus the question, "Are you a good
witch or a bad witch? And no, not all witches are ugly. Everyone has
powers. It is how you use your powers that make you a witch.

The Aquarian Age is here to say you need no mediator. Toto acts as
Dorothy's conscience. That is to say as a guide. He is Anubis, who guides
souls through the underworld. By Toto making Dorothy miss the balloon
ride he does her a favor.   It is all hot air anyway. Who wants to hang with a
hot air preacher? Toto is Thoth (Thought). Hot air is not good, she needs to
use her own resources – her silver chord.   Her unconscious mind has a
direct line to God. Her god self is Glinda. Some call it The Higher Self.
Others say it is the Higher Source. But one thing is for sure, we are all
connected to a higher intelligence, whether it manifests as Toto or Glinda.
When this higher intelligence is accessed, some say one has reached the
collective conscience or Akasha.

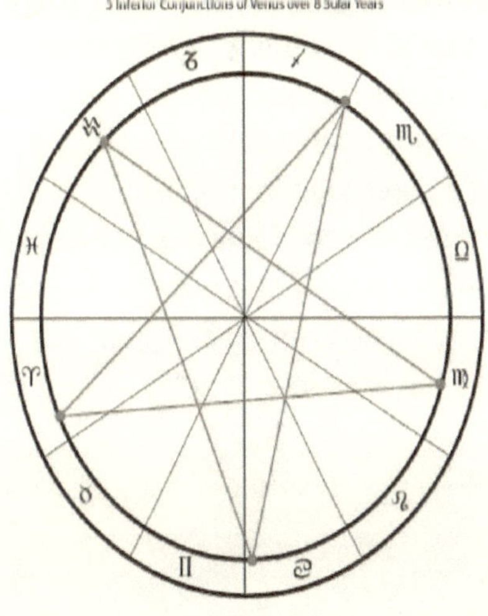

Fairy is another feminine symbol to depict Return of the Goddess or Divine
female Principle. No one is saying males are shams. The people that bring
her back into alignment are males. She needs to shine her light so that
males can become magnetized and shine their light.

Aquarian Age is about unification, not division. In fact, it is the opposite
of division and separation. Under the old system, separation of male and

female was the final call. In Science (as far as the adversary is concerned) the mentality is that things have to be proven in order for people to believe that it exists. As professor Marvel says to Toto as one dog to another. He is making reference to the dog eat dog world of the previous age. Age of Aquarius is here to say, believe in the unseen forces not so much in blind faith of the old school. When you are blind you cannot see or lead.

One has to believe in oneself. Self esteem is an issue Dorothy had. When she wasn't heard, her self esteem was in danger and that is what the sacral Chakra addresses (self esteem). Once one believes in oneself one can be self reliant. When your light shines you cause other's light to shine as well. We learn from each other. Aquarian Age is communal thinking, with focus on what benefits the whole as opposed to what benefits the individual. There are no monopolies that are acceptable in this mentality. Abundance is the key, coming straight from nurturing Mother Nature. Not only are there flowers in Munchkinland but there are fruits that fall from trees in abundance. When Dorothy and her friends get to Emerald City, they are fed. It is always enough for everyone. Lack is a mentality of the old superstitious thinking. It masks itself by calling others superstitious, a reverse psychology so to speak. Abundance thinking is the thinking of a Motherly society. Aquarian thinkers do not believe in man-bashing. The Age of Aquarius embraces men's wisdom. The male and female principle is combined in an alchemy of male and female balance. That is what the liquid represents – al alchemy, a marriage, a coming together of these important energies. Aquarian Age brings attention to what is needed to solve problems.

In the tarot, we see the angel of Alchemy. This is the Water Bearer, who mixes a liquid. We also see the Simpleton who begins his journey and has one foot on land and another one on water or over a cliff. This represents being caught up in two worlds, the real and the unreal: That which is tangible and that which is intangible. The fool knows there is more to life just as Dorothy knew there was another life somewhere over the rainbow. She was longing for her Mother. She was an orphan. She was longing for her spiritual Mother. She finds her in Glinda, a protrectress.

Here is a breakdown of the word tarot. Tarot is a word that can be
rearranged to mean different things, but are all related. We find four words
in that one word.   The word means royal path. Torah means law (Moses
law or follow natural law i.e. karma). Orat means prayer. Chants get you
there. In other words, what you wish for can be your heart's desire. Roat
means wheel or road. The wheel of fortune is the wheel of karma. What
goes a-roud, comes around. It is the circle of life and at the same time the
medicine wheel. The phrase "taste your own medicine" would be a good
example of the healing power of karma. Karma can follow you even unto
another reincarnation. Christ incarnated so it's no surprise that humans,
being the sons of god can do the same. The road is the royal path one must
take in order to accomplish one's mission. This is in reference to attaining
one's potential. In the beginning we are a circle of potential; an egg. Get rid
of non-virtuous tendencies under your Zodiac sign and work only on those
high virtues. You have within you virtuous qualities. If you follow the high
road, the world would be a better place. In this case the high road is the
Yellow Brick Road or the Golden Mean or The Golden Rule. Some rule by
might, while others rule with a sane mind. Your light will shine positively
before the world. Otherwise it would glow as a red light, like that of lower
beings such as the evil witch. So you see we are all witches or warlocks or
godlike...ugly witch versus beautiful witch yes we all have power. It is how
you use power that matters. Power in the form of corruption will have
karmic effect; If not in this life maybe the next. Well, let the force be used

properly for we all have access to it. Evil reigns because good people do nothing. While evil appear to be winning, love conquers all. Water is a powerful dissolution of forms. Go Dorothy, state your truth. Dorothy was not one good person who did nothing in the face of evil. Dorothy was one good person who stood up to evil. And that is to be admired.

Finally, Ator is just another name for Hator, an Egyptian goddess that symbolized Mother Earth, a cow-headed goddess, with the sun over the moon. This means she overcame emotions and is a Master. Do you see another goddess of heaven here? I see reincarnation after reincarnation. It is depicted in the

30

Empress as well as many ancient goddesses. She is the symbol of Love and beauty. Another name for Hathor is Hetheru from where hero comes from. There is another allusion to female hero. The munchkins clap at the sight of her as she kills evil. How is that for heroism? Hathor is a very ancient goddess who is also associated with music, dance and other virtues. Many came to the temple of Hathor to have their dreams explained. She is also patroness of the sun.

    A Woman is finally depicted as enlightened in the form of Dorothy. The benevolent heroine who bears a hero/Heru consciousness. Het Heru also means house of Horus. This is the original Christ consciousness. She was a member of royalty and thus ties into the royal path. She is later seen with twin feathers –another allusion to the process of weighing of the heart. Cow goddess were venerated during golden age of the Egyptian Empire. Profesor Marvel is in awe of Osiris and Isis. Isis is another form of Hathor. And how can we forget Taurat, the divine cow goddess. In Greek Thoueris which sounds a lot like DoronThea, means a gift of God. Doron means gift and thea is female god. Taweret was known for being aggressive and Dorothy was super-aggressive as she recites the famous line, "or I'll bite you myself! You wicked old witch!" and hits her! It is said these goddesses are aggressive because they are only protecting their young. Dorothy's baby was Toto. All is symbolic.

Hermes/Tahuti Trimigestus is associated with the Emerald City. We see here that ancient sciences are being alluded to. Dorothy seems to be longing for a time when life was more whole, more colorful or perhaps she wishes she had been born in another era somewhere over the rainbow, where there is no trouble ...people live in peace – a golden age of sorts. Since Tehuti/Hermes is associated with The Emerald City, we pay attention to the concept of three. The word Trimigestus has the number three built into it and alludes to the triple aspect of God. It is a combo of father (Sun) and Holy Spirit which is mother and son/daughter.

   Holy Spirit is part of the trinity. There are 3 companions. Emerald Tablet is an ancient formula that turns green at the end. The heart is key. The green ray...the supreme alchemist is a She?..a worker in the darkness...very deep...resulting in the holy fire aka fiery lion...holy waters (thrown at witch) ...changing into pure and spiritual body..the air or etheric body. Aether is quintessence or 5th element, Dorothy is earth, wind is scarecrow, fire is lion, and water is the Tin-man who is always crying. The story is about transmuting base metal (base qualities in human) into virtuous qualities (gold) thereby reaching another golden age or the phi (the pi) the golden mean, which is perfection. Once Soul is perfectly aligned then it returns to its source, its original path. The planets travel in a path. Everything has its order. In the story one essence has 3 aspects. Judy can be equated to the essence the 5th element who was originally base earth turned or transfigured to gold by following the yellow brick road, the Masonic brick, Egyptian pyramid made of brick. Three companions are her 3 aspects of herself. She is the essence that has 3 aspects, body soul and spirit. They can be likened to earth wind and fire. The air is the essence/quintessence known as the ether. Imhotep himself can be likened to the essence or 5th element. He is the 13th sign. The sun stays in the Serpent Holder's Zodiac for only 19 days. He is the

31

one who healed with symbol of serpent. One has to innerstand esoteric science to overstand the 13th sign. See, Imhotep is the real Wizard. Since Thoth is seen dressed with dog head, the reference is, Toto is The real Wizard. Dorothy follows her dog's lead as you see in the movie as she runs away.

   The journey shows up as a dirt path, going over a bridge, running away, consulting a guru, gazing into ball, facing the rainbow, following a yellow brick road, tapping her shoes = tapping her resources, i.e. tapping into her consciousness. This is the path of a neophyte into adept ship. And Toto leads the way every time. Those who study the Tarot know that the tarot is a story. It is a story about a journey. But many people call it The Royal Path without knowing its true meaning. Well, it is the story of The Royal Path of Innana and her cohorts. Gods and goddesses are known for being of a royal lineage. TheTarot is the book that leads one into one's destiny, one's journey. Few find that path although it has been laid before their eyes. This is because most people have been taught to avoid astrology. The ancient sciences were hidden from the public in order to hide the truth from those who would misuse it. The science itself was never negative but there are those that use natural law for magic that harms others. Ancient sciences are like Pandora's Box in that they can be treated like the Tree of Knowledge of good and evil. Not surprisingly, trees are a part of this ancient story and find their way into Frank Baum's story.

Dorothy utilizes ancient sciences to find answers to her problem.   Finally, she relies on herself as her guides has been telling her all along. One guide is Toto or Anubis, god of underworld. Dogs are seen in dreams.   At the end, The Wizard takes on the role of Anubis saying a man's heart is measured not by how much he loves but by how much he is loved by others. This reminds us that Anubis also carries a scale in order to weigh the hearts of those who have passed. The Process of Weighing the Heart meant that a person's bad deed should not outweigh their good deed. The good deeds you do have to do with what kind of heart you have if you have.. So Toto behaves in the same way that Anubis does in the ancient writings.   Toto appears to be guiding Dorothy in her journey through what can be considered the underworld since she is knocked unconscious. There are double meanings. Her being knocked unconscious makes reference to how women fell asleep in a world dominated by males, and forgot how to use their powers. But there is help for Dorothy besides Toto.

Her other guide is Glinda, the good fairy, her higher self , the Mother Goddess the Divine Feminine Principle. The word principle is used to describe this energy. It signifies that in all things there are male and female energies. Polarity comes to mind. In a twist of irony Dorothy becomes polarized. Dorothy lives in a by-gone era, is an orphan and yearns for her mother. She connects to Female Divinity after she goes within. In her journey she finds answers . In essence Dorothy after losing her voice finds her voice after having a deep transformation. The event happens at the cusp of the Piscean Age and Aquarian Age. The virtues of Aquarian Age include freedom, independence, self reliance, sharing and inclusiveness. That is to say, Aquarius represents what is best for the whole. Her companions are male and attain wisdom. Dorothy aligns her Chakras as she goes through her inner journey.   The Kundalini serpentine fire comes out and she is able to see better and think better. The earlier immature fits and tantrums are a thing of the past. We watch her grow up literally. She realizes that no matter how far

32

one travels, home is still where the heart is. And she can't go looking for her heart's desire elsewhere. This means you can't go looking for yourself in other people's culture. This is being true to self. Know thyself applies here. Much wisdom originates in ancient mystery schools. At a very famous temple are inscribed words that carry the same message. Even in times of Christ there were mystical secret orders such as The Essenes. Not only do we hear this "know thyself" proverb in ancient Egypt, but it carries to Israel as well. Then it eventually finds its way to the West.

Unfortunately though, a science had to be suppressed due to persecution. But this science is now being brought to the forefront in the Age of Aquarius. The Age of Aquarius is The Age of Revelation, where not one stone is left unturned. All low life will be exposed. Some people are afraid of this Age. Like a cowardly lion, we fear the unknown. What we can learn from the lion is this.   Face your fears and stop spooking things out. Behind every magic, there is a science. We have to learn to be courageous if we are to attain our destiny. When the witch and Dorothy made comments about the hourglass being almost empty that is a true statement. Aquarius is halfway in time from a complete circle. This means we have yet to experience Capricorn, Libra, Scorpio and others. So that makes us young ladies and gentlemen or middle aged. In terms of evolution, we are just now maturing as a planet. If you don't know yourself, someone else can use your sciences against you and turn you into a slave or a captive audience. Either way it is no good. As much preaching and attending church as some people have done, how far has it gotten them? It certainly has not created resources. This is not to say turn against spirituality. This is to say turn against religion. Conmen live there. There is no currency in religion unless it belongs to the preacher. But in spirituality your currency gets you everything you want.

The real question is why was the science suppressed? Naturally when you go around enslaving people, you are not going to want them to know who they are or else they would free themselves. First you have to make believe the captured people are inferior. It is all a clever use of psychology. In the storyline, we see ramifications of enslavement in the cry for independence of the munchkins. These "little" people represent the Ptahites erroneously called pygmies or Black people in general who were captured. Interestingly enough, it was the Ptah that gave birth to the Putah or Buddha, the enlightened one also known as The Black One.

Blind obedience to religious heads is necessary for the system to work. Even Dorothy herself is captured just as royal lines and nobles in Africa and in the West were later captured right along with everyone else. In the Tarot card this is depicted by The Devil Card, who not surprisingly has chains in his hands. A picture is worth a thousand words. And that is exactly the intention of The Tarot deck, which is none other than the Little Book that is open, has no beginning or end. No one knows if it ends with the world or start with the World Card, or The Simpleton. The same situation happens with astrology. No one can figure out if it begins with Aries or Virgo, the Virgin, or Leo, the king and so on. Maybe even Cancer, the ancient mother, the lunar dynasty. Anything that is circular has no beginning, nor end. Taurus is sometimes called the Omega and Alpha due to the shape of the sign. Whether this is making reference to Egypt, The Zep Tepi which means first time, is unknown. One thing is for sure. Zep Tepi is an Egyptian term referring to the first time that the gods came down to Earth and created The Golden

33

Age among other things. The author wonders if the Golden Calf has anything to do with this. Either way, circles have no beginnings, nor ends. So anyone with a logical mind may be able to argue all of the above. But either way, we are left with one thought. And that is, how will Dorothy and her pals save the day?

From the Scarecrow we learn the importance of using the brain. It has been said that humans only use 1 tenth of their brain. Considering all the distractions that should not be surprising. The distractions keep one from concentrating on spirituality. In real life people are preoccupied with the mundane because the material world is holding them hostage. One does not need to look too far to see that the land has been high-jacked, along with the water, fire and air. These four elements are precisely what the four main characters represent. Dorothy is Earth, very practical and is associated with foundation or home. That is also describing one of the four signs that comprise the end time characters, which is Taurus. The Scarecrow is Air represented as an airhead. The Lion, Leo is fiery or fire and the Tin-man is Water. So there you have it. The four elements have been high-jacked. Today we have to pay for all four of these elements, whereas once upon a time it was free for all and unheard of to highjack nature. Proof that the elements have been compromised lies in all the diseases we face today. The people are sick just as Dorothy and her pals were sick or perceived themselves as sick or lacking in something. When you are ruled by tyrants and a single authority deprived of divinity, it is no wonder. In the story, we see these elements being high-jacked in the form of the kidnapping that took place of these characters by the witch and her monkeys. The monkeys represent the lower astral plane as well as agents who are part of the oppressed group but find it easier to work for evil even if it means oppressing your own in the process. This group of people is lazy and part of the seven deadly sins because it leads nowhere. The person does not attain their destiny while preventing others from reaching their destiny. Many scriptures speak of these Fence Straddlers. Agents hold people prisoners just as witches and religious fanatics do. The problem with religious fanatics is that they too, prevent others from attaining their potential. Anytime you have to convert someone while acting ugly like the Gatekeeper, then you know something is wrong. That is the ultimate form of hypocrisy. Churches fill one potential. And that is the preacher's pocket. People need to let others come into their own and let others think for themselves. Four characters will save the day. Four types of people will save the day in the end. You can find these characters in the Sphinx.

The author thinks that the Scarecrow represents the eagle, being that it flies through the air. A lot of speculations can be made from this wonderful movie. These four signs form the Sphinx, the four people that will save the day in the last day and times. In other words if the people stop being scared and would use their brain and stop killing each other, develop a heart, their chakras would open and they would be able to solve their own problems and find their way home. So there you have it; the riddle of the Sphinx has been solved. People have to take on these characteristics, if they are to lead the way into the new Era. You must be perseverant as an ox/bull, courageous as a lion, ethereal as an eagle and grounded as a human.

34

It is hard to tell if Frank Baum was aware of the many interpretations that a book can have, especially his. Did he mean for this? Was he a genius? This is one of those books that lend itself to many interpretations. Perhaps it is because it is rooted in reality. Historical accounts simply shed light into what is happening. This book or movie appears to be an account of history. The history of a spaceship that landed and got destroyed and the aliens made Earth their home. In the process of existing, they were seen as gods considering their advance technology. In fact Tehuty of ancient times was also called Techu from which the word technology came from. Clearly ancient people were way more advanced than the so-called modern man. If anyone has read the story of Innana and how her jewels were removed as she travelled in a circle, one can't help but picture how the African female was stripped of all her clothes despite her royal status. Ironically she is the object of worship as The Black Madonna amongst those who know. She is also worshipped as the goddess Venus, the well shaped figurine taken with her African curvy figure. Being that original cultures were matrilineal, it should not surprise anyone as to what the author was trying to say. But these things had to be done delicately or it would upset the status quo. So it had to be done in a story form. These are after all, the people who confiscated artifacts, burned down libraries and claimed others' legacy. Perhaps Frank Baum was not part of that and simply stumbled upon the information, as a man of privilege who was a writer and had access to information.

It is not far-fetched to imagine a goddess feeling homesick, being light-years away from home and all. The circular motion in the story portrays karma at its best and how life and time or the universe period operates in a circle. No one knows exactly how old the earth is but we do know that cycle repeat themselves in the form of seasons, night and day. There is evidence of orbits and all spheres are circular.

So in real life we learn that certain Ages were characterized by certain personalities. Earlier we discussed writing, communication, mother cultures, father cultures and the upcoming androgynous Age which is predominantly female as the Divine Mother is once again acknowledged in this divine cycle of time. It is quite necessary that this happens because generally when women rule there are less wars, if any. And there is peace and harmony. Female Energy as well as Aquarian thinking is characterized by inclusivity. This is true of matriarchies as well as African societies when they are not exposed to foreigners. Go back to antiquity and you see that the beginning was nothing like now. Anyone who is honest with themselves knows that females are nurturing by nature. In fact that's why people call nature Mother, because mothers are nurturing and are in tune with nature. Not only do they have cycles as in the natural world but they are also intuitive. They go within. This is a Divine right of women, to be their god selves and find the answers within. Because female headed societies are egalitarian, they are not generally oppressive to men as are patriarchal societies.

The Wizard of Oz makes a good point in pointing this out. It shows males as tyrants or overbearing, including the Wizard and The Gatekeeper. It does show bad witches. So yes, just as some males are not aligned, some women are not aligned. Many people regardless of gender can be out of balance. But the point is that male dominated religion is shown in the Wizard as one that is overbearing and intolerant,

unquestionable, everyone running around in fear, mindlessly dependent. Aquarian female thinking is just the opposite. It is characterized by independence in the sense of freedom....freedom for all. It is sovereignty. Glinda on the other hand has just the opposite demeanor. She looks and acts serene and lets others learn on their own. That's a true goddess. This is the side of god that we should all embrace.   If the Earth is to survive this is a must. If the trees are to stop being chopped this is a must. For the sake of the survivorship of the earth we must embrace mother and a mother culture.

Frank Baum needs to be congratulated for bringing forth images of mother earth/ mother goddess. Mother Nature is divine female principle. Thank you Baum for letting us become aware of the other side of God. As we try to perfect ourselves by aligning our Chakras we get rid of negative energies such as hatred, envy, anger, aggressiveness and so on. The time for immaturity is up and it is time to grow up. The Chakras themselves are circular. Also they move in a circular motion. Is it any wonder the author utilizes circles to emphasize the feminine aspect of God. Nature is at its best producing fruits and lovely colorful flowers along with rainbows. There is no way this all could be a coincidence. Frank Baum uses imagery and symbols and storylines to depict the divine feminine. After we come across this story we should realize that we can reach the Divine directly ourselves, without intermediaries .